MW01594753

CHASING THE TRUTH

Lisa Kahl

Copyright © 2020 Lisa Kahl.
All rights reserved.

No part of this book may be reproduced in any manner without the
written consent of the publisher except for brief excerpts in critical
reviews or articles.

ISBN: 978-1-7923-4589-0

Printed in the United States of America.

ISBN 978-1-7923-4589-0

90000>

DEDICATION

I dedicate these pages to my past.

I love you with all of my heart and I thank you for all of your lessons.

I will carry the memories and the wisdom you have bestowed upon my soul,

as I embark into a future full of service, full of gold.

CONTENTS

INTRODUCTION

If

If you are a leaf,

Then I am a tree,

I among you and you among me.

If you are a drop,

Then I am a shower,

Of friendship's rain to grow bond flower.

If you are a ripple,

Then I am a river,

 A current of love to heal heartbreak's shiver.

If you are a rainbow,

then I am the sky,

One in the same, in soul, you and I.

Little Bird of Clare

Upon a perch, inside a cage,
Built by years of pent up rage,
Little bird of sunny yellow,
Called on oak to help her mellow.
Bars of perfection masked as shame,
A never-ending winless game.
Bars of guilt masked as doubt,
Given too much care and clout.
Bars of fear masked as excuses,
Left a trail of defeated bruises.
Then breath by breath, flutter and flap,
Wings had a notion they could zap,
The past, the pain, procrastination,
Fly toward a brighter destination.
Turned her eyes beyond the bars,
Sought heaven's hand among the stars.
Prayed God to lift the latch of door,
For chance to fly again once more.
In spirit, in service, appreciation,
To love, to lead a needy nation.
In gratitude, with grace, devotion,
Shift the gear to forward motion.
East wind blew in and lifted lock,
Door breezed open to my shock!
First paralyzed by need of why,
Of me, of how, of my outcry?

West wind blew in and I accepted,
The Holy Spirit had selected,
This heart of mine and feather's true,
Christ had work for me to do.
I took the leap and opened wide,
No longer would I ever hide,
Behind the mishaps life did fashion,
Would channel them into compassion,
For every soul in need of love,
From little bird sent from above.

SUPPRESSED

Golden Butterfly

Battered, beaten down by life,
Single mom and betrayed wife.
Injured body, low self-esteem,
Smile turned to frown from beam.

Shattered, hopeless, lost in space,
Enclosed heart in locked up case.
Nowhere to go, no one to listen,
No chance to cure lonely condition.

Pills for depression, wine for sleep,
World's way to cope when in too deep.
Or so it seemed until one day,
Sweet butterfly did come my way.

Led to a space of peace and quiet,
Far cry from scene of bar and riot.
Foreign to me this healing practice,
With power to mend a human cactus.

Yoga? Breathing? Namaste?
Is this work or is this play?
What on earth is going on?
Room wrapping me in white chiffon.

Just when I thought it couldn't get better,
Teacher sailed in like bottled letter.
A mystery she was to me,
Seemed so at ease to let all be…

Just as they are, be it strong or shaken,
In such acceptance, my soul was taken,
By this angel of God with halo hair,
Tilted head and sincere stare.

Still water voice so soft and clear,
"Welcome, I'm so glad you're here."
Cue the music, dim the light,
Her essence shone, her gifted sight…

Entered bodies in the space,
Free of judgement, full of grace.
Words spoken to my deepest fears,
Secrets, ramblings, held for years.

As if she tiptoed in my mind,
Unafraid of what she'd find.
Exposed the pain left unexpressed,
The anger I had long repressed.

Tucked tight in ball in back left corner,
She dared sharp spines as grief reformer.
A touch not from a hand but wing,
Brought tears to surface, skin to sing!

Who knew my body could succumb,
To touch of love while still so numb?
Time off the carousel of pain,
Shelter from abusive rain.

Cocooned by golden butterfly,
Rocked by her gentle lullaby.
Treasured ground to heal and grow,
Surrendered self did come to know...

We shared a field of light, compassion,
One day The Lord would bless and fashion,
Fresh start, dew floor, manicured and mowed,
And send us down the yellow brick road.

Blow the Horn

How will I ever get this out?
The past abuse denied its shout.
Time has come to blow the horn!
Brush the anger and the scorn!
Strokes of sickness in the head,
Trapped by another's rage I bled.
Under regime of mind control,
Imprisoned by his watch patrol.
Held hostage in a vault of fear,
A shadow of the self in mirror.

One Last Look

One last look, one last goodbye,
Despair Dad's leaving in a sigh.
Burden now shall fall on me,
To care for Mom in misery.
Set the tone for rest of life,
To take on other's grief and strife.
Screen door slammed as he did exit,
Along with gifts inside my basket.
An end to melodies in hall,
Piano abandoned by shocked heart's wall.
Walls designed to keep me small,
To keep me safe and free from fall,
Of diving in myself too deep,
Of owning voice beyond girl's peep,
Of owning talents in the arts,
Of music, writing, reading hearts.
A dismal day when soul gives way,
To other's problems, feelings, blaze.
Allows their essence to be snuffed out,
Self-confidence be crushed by doubt.
For had Dad realized the repercussions,
Perhaps more effort in salvage discussions.

Lakes of Sorrow

Rubber bands pull down on legs,
Ease compression so body begs.
Pail of poetry resides in center,
The landlord God, as story renter.
What is it that You have to say?
When will this pain ever give way?
Pressure building, beaker breaks,
Upheaval of this lady's lakes.
Lakes of secrets, lakes of sorrow,
Lakes of truths for victim's borrow.
Wisdom from a painful past,
When spirit crushed by bully cast.
A wretched time as I fell prey,
To stalker's snare throughout the day.
Unstable mind of alcoholic,
Attacks of nature diabolic.
Haunt of hunt for years ensued,
Result a melancholic mood.
For how much can one woman take,
When faced with infinite heartbreak?
Tremors sewn inside her dress,
Anxiety, post-traumatic stress.
Nightmares, sweats, unsafe at home,
No retreat to call her own.
Afraid to speak, to take a part,
Upset the family apple cart.
A cry for help so deeply buried,
Best for this girl to stay unmarried.

Bed of Nails

Bed of nails as one adjusts,

To consequences earned from lust.

Truth will find its way to shine,

Only remains a matter of time.

Anticipation of confession,

Carves abyss of chest depression.

An elephant with bricks on feet,

Stomps on body in defeat.

To lighten load and breathe again,

Soul must cleanse the mortal sin.

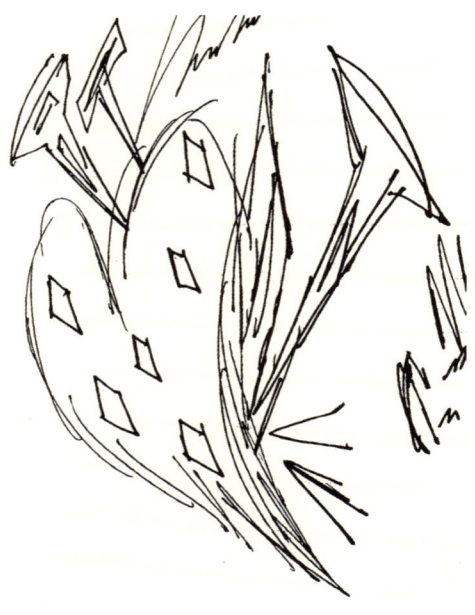

Holes

Holes in the story, holes in the bed,

Holes in a once contented head.

Holes in the heart, holes in the stomach,

Holes in life's cockpit cause plunder and plummet.

Holes in the eyes, holes in the ears,

Holes in the lies he's been telling for years.

Holes in the hands, holes in the wrists,

Holes punctured from finally grasping his trysts.

Hole wounds in vagina, hole wounds in the hip,

Hole wounds in desire of sex sinking ship.

Hole craters in legs, hole tunnels in knees,

Whole amputation to end the pain please.

Holes in the ankles, holes in the feet,

Holes in the step of past partnership beat.

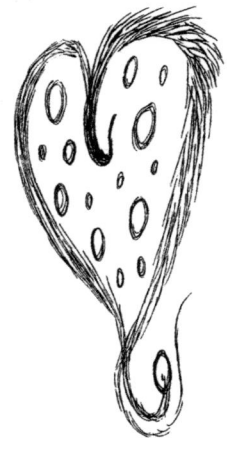

Encased

Encased inside hard chestnut shell,

Too tough to crack the victim's spell,

The abuse cycle a machine,

Set to spin, did steal my scream.

Shoo Fly

Shoo fly don't bother me,

Nor pie of mediocrity,

T'was baked so many years ago,

Is comforting, is all I know.

A River Runs

A river runs upon the sleeve,

Current creeping to upheave,

Limb of lust, stench of sin,

Crawling through each pore of skin.

Oh waterway of love and light,

Wash away a heart contrite.

Crystallize God's holy virtue,

Sanctify me, of this i urge you.

Reform offense, repair the wreckage,

Hail on me angelic message.

Prudence, peace and purity,

Recruit respectability.

Of this I know, of this I vow,

Rectitude from toe to brow.

Blood transfused by His redemption,

Sinner to saint by His correction.

Shrapnel

Feathers stuck to built up walls,

Shrapnel caused by empty calls.

Promises in vain, all broken,

A parting gift, unwanted token.

How was it that I did believe?

His every word and charming deed.

His warm embrace all lies of lace,

A treasured bond was not the case.

When will I ever finally learn?

To shelve false union in the urn.

Burn the memories into dust,

Reclaim self from man a must.

Bottoms Up

Sip, sip, sip to kill the pain,

The ridicule and disdain.

Swig, swig, swig to lobotomize,

Memory of love and all that dies.

Chug, chug, chug to hide the loss,

Of self-esteem, belief in cross.

Drown, drown, drown inside the bottle,

Road of despair, foot at full throttle!

Stricken

One day I've rainbows in my veins,
The next mud puddles from the rains,
Of life's surprises we don't see coming,
Grief of loss quicksand, mind numbing.

Why must humans feel this pain?
Be whisked in bowl that's far from sane.
Flipped upside down and inside out,
Stripped of varnish, chipped of grout.

Clear the Decks

Clear the decks, clear the body,

Clear the throat and drink truth toddy.

Speak up, speak out, speak around the world,

Of mystery that has unfurled.

You need not fear of who you are,

You need not fear to shine as star.

To hold it in, internalize,

Body tremors, tears swell in eyes.

The time has come to let it go,

Let it be and let it show.

Some will believe and some will not,

Pay no attention, just take your shot.

Surrounded you shall be by guides,

Protected, led and mystified.

From your smile joy will spread,

From your story new life to dead.

Enough Already

Hold us to your breast bluebird,
Fair feathered wings banish absurd,
Demand, control of the dictator,
Dark energy of complicator.

For we flew the nest to begin anew,
Yet still entangled by cuckoo.
How many miles will it take,
To have fair share, to claim our stake?

Go on fear fowl, step on love's feet,
Peck precious heart, poke wisdom's beak.
Hoard seed for self in vile greed,
Only takes one to make flock bleed.

A true leader leads from the behind,
Cheers on weakest in step and climb.
To share the sun on top of mountain,
Joins forces in abundance fountain.

Safe Mode

Body shut down but for a while,
Set to safe mode, lost its smile.
Tremored in fear, cried out in rage,
Grief and torment took front stage.
Pain all over, nerves run amuck,
Spirit in quicksand, compressed and stuck.
Anxious, depressed and disconnected,
Until one day she recollected,
Of where she came from, her family genes,
Tough as nails and full of dreams.
Called out in plea to all those past,
Gift me courage, break hell's cast.
Drop down from heaven a glitter of Dad,
A sliver of Grandpa to release my sad.
The strength of Grandma who was a rock,
A tenacious mother and building block.
Heal my soul, restore my mind,
Remove me from the push and grind.
Of doctor's, meds, of fear and doubt,
For I am ready now to sprout.
Be not afraid to grow alone,
As my own temple of Holy Throne.
Become as strong as weeping willow,
Legs strong as trunk, heart soft as pillow.
From glory to glory I shall go,

With God beside me and Dad in tow.

SEVERED

Trappings

Before the break of naïve blood,

Housed in a heart of tender mud,

Lived petals of a purple dream,

Of a marriage born beside a stream.

Barefoot beginning in crystal current,

Baptism by nature the finest deterrent,

Of the trappings of a heedless culture,

Devil of connection and relationship vulture.

The dime, the drive, the work of men,

While women's attention on family and friend.

The hearth, the home, what truly matters,

Yet success be defined when the glass ceiling shatters.

Perhaps feel these words and take what you will,

Drop out of the rat race, lay perfectly still.

Is your life the way you dreamed it would be?

The answer resides in the stream and the tree.

Tides of Lies

Tides of lies washed ashore,

Muddied sand once white and pure,

Flipped wholesome seashells upside down,

Sent steady seagulls spinning round.

Obey the Rules

Trying to obey the rules, take the pills as building tools,

Reform the mind, reconstruct the body,

Although the soul left feeling shoddy.

I so often wonder is this the way?

To numb myself throughout the day?

Half alive feels dead to me,

In haze of drugs it's hard to lead,

A household, child, a class, a venture,

All joy and emotion now have a censor.

Mind as well be strapped to table,

Essence is no longer able,

To shine, to speak, to move, to grow,

This is not living of this I know.

When will this veil of sorrow lift?

And I be given precious gift,

Of my true nature, free and wild,

Pure innocence of wondrous child!

How much more must I endure?

I've had my fill of this I'm sure!

Seeped

Seeped through the brick, the wall and the floor,

Confusion, flirtation behind every door.

Intimate moments with beautiful ladies,

Dose of ego and lust tipped the scales end of weighty.

Soiled

A soiled space in need of scrubbing,

Confession sponge for purity rubbing.

Wrongdoing of humanity,

Stained the holy ground indeed.

One's actions leave their fingerprint,

Clog air with film of dense sin lint.

Over time the residue,

Detracts our friends, they bid adieu,

For cleaner pastures free of muck,

Flee muddy waters of those stuck.

Wish them well but carry forward,

Self-love a savior for untoward,

Behavior that does not align,

With who you are at such said time.

Fairy Dip

A fairy dip in fog-eyed river,

Purge clit from man who made her quiver,

Plead oak and willow to forgive her,

Cleanse wings and womb for babe's deliver.

Godspeed

A heart in a wing had been waiting to sing,

Poetic words to soften the sting,

Of the end of two lovers who did try their best,

To reignite passion and peace to their nest.

Best efforts were made from deep in the bone,

Still, love lost in the stars, not set in the stone.

Adrift from the other, shook up in the head,

A deep knowing it's time to put it to bed.

Cover old story and take off the rings,

Godspeed and sweet dreams to these angel wings.

Heartache

Have you ever felt like you're the one?

Basked in the sun of kingdom's come?

Only to find in teardrops river,

No matter made about your quiver.

End of Days

The end of days when we connected,

In truth I now feel quite rejected.

It's gone as far as it can go,

Thermostat is far below,

The temperature it takes to heat,

Two souls to fill the marriage seat.

Engine sputtered, fire to ember,

Yet all my days I shall remember,

The love, the friendship, the comradery,

The tender true story of you and me.

Confess

Shattered glass, shards of secrets,

Stripped and sliced love's dimension, deepness.

Bed be made, a two-timing mess,

Time has come to cough up, confess!

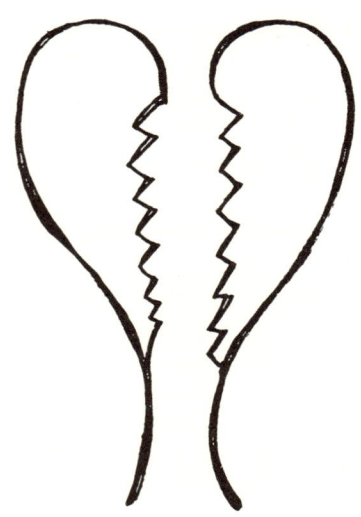

Despair

Seething anger, purple bruises,
An affair where everybody loses.
Splattered bodies on the road,
As details begin to unfold.
Vomit stricken, stirred and shaken,
Breathless for there's no mistaken,
Adultery has shattered marriage,
Violated a family with disparage.

Imminent Death

Lanced for life to heal the strife,

Despair from broken man and wife.

Send heart of hea ing energy,

Through prayer of Mary's rosary.

The pain he feels, you too once felt,

The burn, the sting of divorce pelt.

Too much to take, too much at stake,

The never-ending lawyer's rake.

The knowing now the end is final,

Internal scream in gut be primal.

A marriage on the chopping block,

Awaits the guillotine's death clock.

The Chamber

The night becomes love's memory chamber,

Throughout divorce, life's rearranger.

What's been a process, now an event,

As one spouse soon becomes hellbent,

To put a stop to the frustration,

No longer bound by dedication,

To make it work, no longer goal,

To fit square peg inside round hole.

Now sleepless nights to stare at ceiling,

Try bargaining, the wheeling-dealing.

Begging God to flip a switch,

Go back in time, repair the ditch.

One's body comes apart at seams,

In flushing of one's hopes and dreams.

No greater failure felt indeed,

Then witnessing your children bleed,

As Mom and Dad do seal the deal,

The situation all too real.

Limits pushed, it's run its course,

Papers drawn for pair's divorce.

The time's now come and cut through bone,

It's time now to let it alone.

The Willows

I took to the willows,

To weep deep with me,

For trust that was shattered,

Where once harmony.

A space I held sacred,

Shadow did descend,

Hypocrisy, ego,

Around every bend.

Shiny on surface,

Yet hollow in root,

Heart triggered soul,

To give us the boot!

Fly away little bird,

So you can grow big,

Become one with the leaf,

The branch and the twig.

To own Divine's voice,

To build a truth mansion,

Nest and prepare,

'Tis time for expansion.

Toucan

Once it hit, boy what a smack!
Freight train ran right off the track.
Lights went on, flame did burn,
Bucket of secrets began to churn.

Most close the eyes, don't stir the pot,
Pain of the truth feels like gunshot!
Allow the wounds to grow, continue,
'Til one speaks up and says, "Me too."

Last piece in place of seductive puzzle,
Released the jaw of groomer's muzzle,
Little bird's beak turned toucan's bill,
From tweet to squawk to end his thrill.

Detour

Perhaps not the end but only a detour,

As waves of grief crash onto seashore.

With foam of hope to mend the fences,

Restore the peace, let down defenses.

Find way back into the huddle,

Kinship circle free of muddle.

Regain the trust, an uphill climb,

For you do the crime, you do the time.

Emerald Drops

Emerald drops to heal the pain,

Of goodbye's crack and heartbreak's rain.

Some departures happen twice,

Second loss a deeper slice.

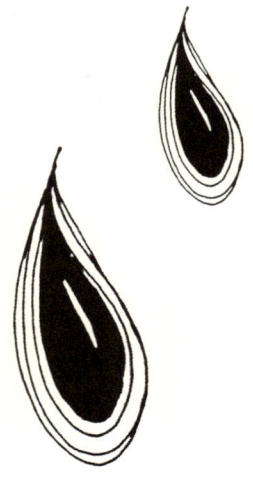

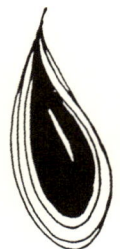

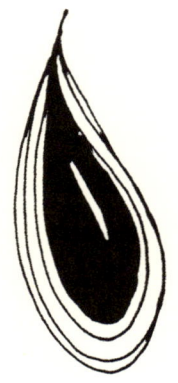

Severed

Exhausted by the this and that,

The tug of war of divorce hat,

The give, the take, the bend, the break,

The amount of money that is at stake.

Vitriolic statements of those we love,

Heavy hits from lawyer's glove.

Shared parenting versus custody,

Support of child's agency.

The hapless system, the wreck-less gavel,

Front row seat to life's unravel.

Family members now a number,

Set schedules that shall encumber,

Holidays, school recitals,

Summer vacations, on time arrivals

Devastations to each soul,

Ironically peace was the goal.

Crimson Tears

First a drip, then a drop,

Faucet heart leaked red nonstop.

Crimson tears for all the years,

I gifted phony, fickle peers.

Believed their fort a special place,

Blessed with gratitude and grace.

Came to find right from the start,

Friends til we do dollar part.

Tourniquet

Tourniquet to cut the flow,

Of divorce blood from pore to toe.

Each step out door of home and child,

A brand to join other's exiled.

Tail in a trap of right versus wrong,

Squeezed between a conscience prong.

Failure pounds at covenant's door,

Vows once made shall be no more.

Excruciating pain ensues,

Far beyond past break up blues.

Such heavy weight to split a family,

Pressed dents in hearts, a true calamity.

Slamming Door

Slamming door on dream's bouquet,

Closing lock on fateful day,

The one arrived to dance and play,

Scribe a story, come what may,

Of love from past, of love today,

Of love eternal, here to stay.

Perhaps in century to come,

He'll conquer fear that makes him run.

In getting out of his own way,

Will win the girl for heart's hooray!

SURRENDER

In the Wings

Waited in the wings for the one to arrive,

Unsteady, unsure of what I'd derive.

Sacred space felt like satin,

My voice it did flatten,

Heart shook in the knowing,

Soul soon would be growing.

Entered God's vessel, masked as a man,

Took seat beside me, so began the grand plan.

"Why are you here?" he questioned this lamb.

I replied, " I don't think I know who I am."

I remember the grin that curled on his face,

Only to vanish without word and or trace.

To the table he led me to lay it all down,

Time had come to surrender life's heavy crown.

For a girl with such fear of men in command,

First miracle happened feeling safe in his hand.

Flat on my back, eyes straight to the ceiling,

Vulnerable, motionless, open book to all healing.

Who was this man with hands of light, hands of love?

Touch of hope, grace and freedom from the Lord up above.

Curiosity nibbled to turn my gaze toward him,

Found him off in a trance with my surface to skim.

Twas if he was watching a movie play out,

I the star actress on the big screen without,

Any care that he see what had happened to me,

What I'd done, who I was, who I knew I could be.

But it was when he looked down right into my eyes,

That my soul left my body leaving me to surmise,

His presence empowered my spirit to roam,

As if God was above me, as if I'd found home.

I am

I am who I am, this is the simple truth,

Let go of the jitters, accept peace filled booth.

It's waiting for you to take a seat and relax,

Let go of the pressure of how one reacts,

To your strength, to your joy, to your essence and ploy,

To serve God on life's stage, so stop playing coy.

You get ever so close to your full potential,

Then pull back and retreat, defer existential.

Your presence is needed, your voice should be heard,

Uncoil yourself from the pain, it's absurd!

Tip

Words to tip him right side up,

Break the pattern, interrupt,

A coping habit used for years,

Time to shift the needy gears.

hope

truth

love

Words to the Page

Words to the page,

Unleash the rage,

Of waters below,

Full of words with orange glow.

Jot one, then the next,

'Tis a joy, not a test,

A communion with God,

His path you do trod.

As you let it all out,

Free of guilt, free of doubt.

The pen be your savior,

Of bad belly's behavior,

Too much in the gut,

Release all, strut your stuff!

The time now has come,

To face and not run,

From the truths you've discovered,

Nurtured and mothered,

Alone in your nest,

In your soul at its best,

Sleep snug as a bug,

Tomorrow well's dug.

Unfold

Body slips, whispers break,

Feet a flutter, heart a quake,

Skin sails freedom painted gold,

In Hands of God thou doth unfold.

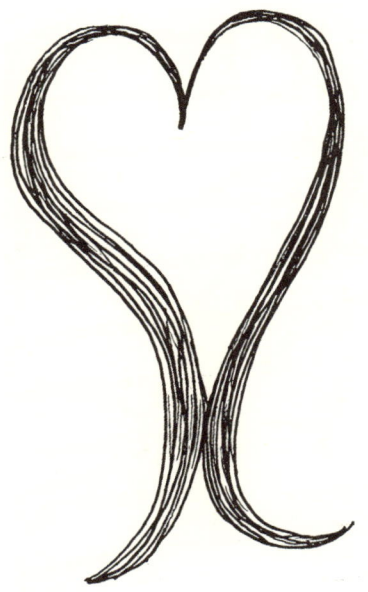

Dear God,

Show me what I need to see,

Make it of you and not of me.

True to Self

Sword of petal, bud and vine,

Embolden heart be true to Thine.

Pump Up Your Chest

Pump up your chest,

Let it fly,

To hold it in,

Just makes you cry.

Repressed anger spells depression,

Time to spill a full confession.

Game is over, jig is up,

You must come clean or risk disrupt,

The forming of a pair rock solid,

The second chance, the branch of olive.

Up is Down

Up is down and down is up,

When wine be flowing through the cup,

In vino veritas the phrase,

Truth be told in drunken daze.

Turbulence

Turbulence when man realized,

Ship of secrets was capsized.

Outed, exposed for all to see,

Dropped ego to a humble knee.

Prayed God to show him mercy, grace,

In desperate plea to save some face.

Deep down he knew this time would come,

Stand line of truth, be under gun.

Untethered

Untethered soul to find her way,

Inch by inch she worms through day.

No longer held by any mentor,

She heeds the call of why God sent her.

Control

Control will always have its day,

Yet its energy too dark to stay.

Heart-light will break the bully's cast,

As so many trials, this too shall pass.

Renewed

Years of swallowing excessive sludge,

Coagulated belly fudge,

Of other people's pain and problem,

Feeling I could ease and solve them.

Decades of bricks below the navel,

Blocking self of creative able,

To write, to sketch, to play piano,

To sing my song, a bird soprano.

And then one day I found my mat,

And breath and spirit staged comeback.

Mountain pose, airplane, half-moon,

And confidence began to bloom.

Eagle, dancer, toppling tree,

And balance found way back to me.

Goddess squat and forward fold,

And body felt a letting go.

Savasana and child's pose,

And rest did open heart from close.

Surrounded by my fellow man,

Renewed myself time and again.

Melted blockage, lit a fire,

Reclaimed self for God's desire.

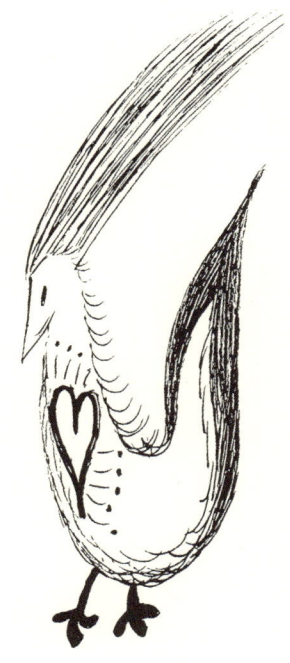

Weeping and Writing

Weeping and writing became the new norm,
As consciousness grew expanding old form.
Sting in the fingers, anger that remained,
Every word dug a grave as it was proclaimed.

Buried the pain the body had carried,
Stress that compressed since the day she got married.
Enough with the sorrow, confusion, abuse,
Granted the pen to let it all loose.

Terror not knowing if she would return,
From the depths of the past, from the scars of the burn.
Humbling to find so many years later,
Anxiety surfaced from time of the traitor.

She trusted the process, kept at it, kept going,
In between sobs the poems began flowing.
Each stanza a healing, a prayer and a kneeling,
Sacrifice and surrender put an end to the reeling.

The chaos, the pressure inside the mind,
The spasm, the pinching crawling up the spine.
The shortness of breath, the spirit of death,
Concern at the end there may be nothing left.

Took a breath and remembered she was wrapped in white light,

Surrounded by angels with her best interest in sight.

This too it shall pass and again I will rise,

After river of tears comes a shell of surprise.

Truth's Web

Charlotte spun a Wilbur web,

Threads of memories long thought dead,

Poked a pig to scribe old story,

Awake the page with allegory.

Feathered pen skipped through nude journal,

First as Private, then as Colonel,

Once trembled words now in command,

Born of God's light within the hand.

Tales of truth in pulse of poem,

Outlined in steps to find way home,

Brick by brick rhyme paved footpath,

To sanctuary of love's bath.

Take a Gamble

Take a gamble, spend some time,

Roll the dice of romance rhyme,

Weave the word's he's waited for,

Dance in his eyes forever.

An Old Friend

I spy an old friend. He's alone in the corner.
Silently sitting like Little Jack Horner.
Set aside for years too many,
The time has come to play aplenty.

First a whisper, then a bark,
He calls to surface from the dark.
"Where have you gone? Where have you been?"
Oh music man return again.

Strum my strings, forget me not,
Replace me to that gentle spot,
Your hands my cradle, your heart my nest,
I crave to be your welcome guest.

God gifted you with musicality,
To sustain a spirit of whimsicality.
As we revive our strong communion,
The blessing be, at long last, reunion.

In exchange for my delayed rebirth,
A buried treasure to unearth.
Together we will woo a lady,
Act the part of the real Slim Shady!

Her knees to buckle, her soul to swoon,
So drop the hammer! Lower the boom!
Rock her top! Turn up the dial!
Unleash her colors and pimp her style!

The benefit will be for all,
Our tune to stretch her ten feet tall.
Each note an inch, each inch a chapter,
Let instrument be lover's captor.

Leave her longing for more, but refusing to grovel,
And her fingers of fire will drip out a novel.

Seashell

Seashell of promise, seashell of dreams,

Seashell of surprises in fated streams.

When will I hold you and rub your rings?

Feel destiny and all it brings?

Peek inside your inner layer?

Where all is clear and all is bare,

For my naked eye to see,

The calling that you have for me.

How Am I?

How am I to fly with broken wings?

To find back flow amidst the sting?

How will I know to find my feet?

Be the black sheep who says, "Bleat, bleat!"

How much longer must I sit?

By self in room, try not to quit.

This test a never-ending story,

Complete this chapter, move to glory.

Floodgates

Once they opened out it came,

The essence of her given name.

Surrendered to her light and God,

Stepped off the ground of abject sod.

Let it flow from hand and heart,

All she'd witnessed from her start,

As youngest sibling, as pregnant teen,

As divorced woman with low self-esteem.

The body no longer could take,

The tremor and resistance shake.

You have a right to tell your story,

Heal your life and heal your body.

Get angry as you recall pain,

Of the past that led to shame.

Spit it out, throw it up,

Do what need be to fill your cup,

With peace of mind and peace of limbs,

Time has come to sink or swim!

Surrender

Surrender the pain to the Highest Order,
Fear not it will pass from your weary shoulder.

Tested to the limit your body has been,
Resurrection of peace will rise once again.

Lean into the healing, fall into the light,
Angels will renew you throughout the night.

Stay close to your Master, Stay close to His mother,
They know and can heal you unlike any other.

The worst now has past yet still residue,
Few more weeks until all is shiny and new.

Sit quiet and pray, sit quiet and breathe,
Trust the Almighty has tricks up His sleeve.

Bear with Me my child, I know it is hard,
Send love with your fingers to all with a card.

HEALING

Rash

A rash of ink to journal spread,

Too much of too much in the head.

Out in plain sight the words demanded,

To be of purpose, eternally branded.

Carved in margins, etched on lines,

To bring about a change in times.

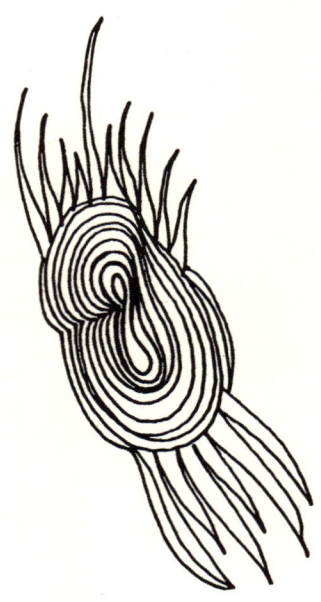

The Blank Page

I'm waiting for you to begin,

To scratch love letter to my skin.

So cold and lonely I have been,

True words will warm my heart again.

Perhaps you think I'm of no feeling,

Am only page of little dealing.

Yet I have traveled round the world,

In novels born from heads that swirled.

Have felt the depths of lover's pain,

Have held disaster and disdain.

Contrary, I was also blessed,

To be a vehicle for zest.

Be first to know of lover's trysts,

Be first to hear of their first kiss!

Ride romance coaster's penmanship,

Unveiling dreams of darling's dip.

Times over since I have been salvaged,

Now bare and ready to be managed,

By novice author such as you,

Who I may teach a thing or two.

Do sit down, grab your favorite pen,

Believe that I am only friend,

To cradle story of your soul,

All is well, of this I know.

Some Days are Diamonds

Some days are diamonds, some days are stones,

Some days the flesh raw that covers our bones.

We drop down to our knees, cry out in mercy,

As soul now is one who is endlessly thirsty,

For the Lord, Jesus Christ, Our Master Creator,

Always our friend, never our traitor.

The Healer of hearts, Sanctifier of spirit,

To Him all the glory, to Him all the merit!

Abundant love each day He shines new,

Pours from His chest to the inside of you.

Accept His peace, answer His call,

The time is now, no need to stall.

Rainbow's End

Sit quiet with God throughout your pain,

Stay clear, stay calm and let it rain.

Your rainbow waits to shine again,

Each time brighter round the bend.

In Repair

Although in repair you still have purpose,

Stay humble and hopeful instead of discouraged,

With a positive outlook and belief in the self,

You are able to play this hand you were dealt.

Overcome evil's snare, keep jumping each hurdle,

No matter if pace is as slow as a turtle.

Forward in thought and away from the sadder,

Until finish line and heart of the matter.

Sit Down

Sit down, sit down, today's for stillness,
Backyard enough to cure your illness.
The coverage of the pines your blanket,
Foliage warm soup to comfort… take it,
Out of body, give it to Earth,
Recycle it for your rebirth.
Trees still barren of their leaves,
Yet as they fill in they're sure to please,
Your readiness to regain health,
Freedom to dance, to fill yourself.
Grass still patchy, growth uneven,
As is your growth which leaves you reeling.
Nature accepts the forward, backward,
Moves through with grace and not a word.
Soft hue of bark softens the skin,
Enough to allow fresh air in.
Blue skies paint throat with worthy song,
What you say matters, there's nothing wrong,
With singing truth, with singing sorrow,
With singing blessings for a better tomorrow.
Last year's dead leaves being cleared out,
Of bed's and bushes for new to sprout.
In the ground to grow the need,
To be a little cherry tree,
Who one day will help the world to see,
Life is but a bowl of joy!
To live and laugh, simply enjoy!

Reconnecting

Reconnecting at base of spine,

Tingling nerves do take their time.

They run the show and won't be rushed,

Test the mind to not be crushed.

For none of us can rush our healing,

Best we can do is take to kneeling,

Ask our Creator to hold us steady,

Until the body decides it's ready,

To step into new role and live,

It's second act, God's gift to give.

See God

I see God everywhere I go,

In tiny pebbles cast ashore.

In rippled seashells on the floor,

Of ocean clear enough to see,

The Lord in all, the Lord in me.

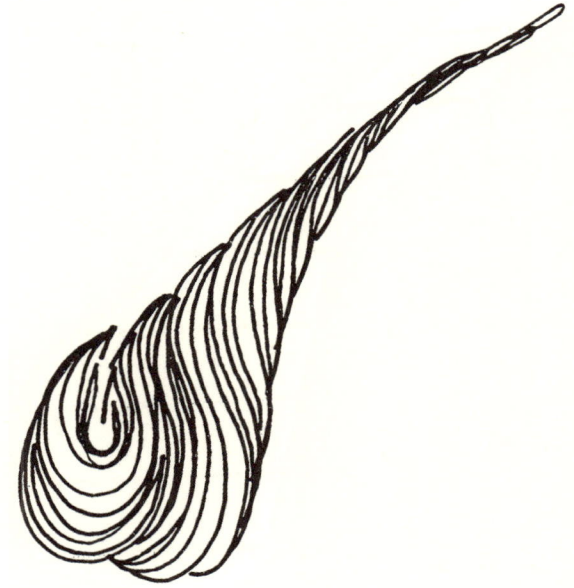

Woodland

Away in the woodland,

Amid daffodils,

Surrendered to soil,

Eye gazing sky's thrills.

I listen to petals,

Who speak dear to me,

Who trumpet the truth,

Of all I can be.

Dandelion

Slinked in the soft and dewy grass,

To pick a daisy from the mass,

Of tumbleweeds and tulips blue,

Of dandelions who never grew,

To full potential as they should,

To see their worth, they never would.

Until one rainy Sunday morn,

Sun poured in to save forlorn,

Weeds that thought they were beneath,

Fancy flowers in the heap,

Of hills and plains and riverbed,

Of badlands, landscape of bare thread.

Rays of warmth, illumination,

Full of encouragement, determination,

To help a dandelion see itself,

As the gold it is, to know its wealth.

Lost Girl

Lost girl at sea, no hope in sight,
Clung to buoy with all her might!
Waves of madness, waves of grief,
Waves as tall as mountain steep.
Her teeth chattered, her legs did shake,
Her life she thought for sure they'd take.
Then father's voice rang in her ear,
Her heart he hoping for to steer,
"Lisa, no risk and no reward,"
So girl began to swim for shore.
Let go of old and tired ways,
People, places that had seen their days.
Took breath of courage, stretched arms wide,
Kicked and splashed her way through tide.
Terrified, alone in dark,
Lord keep me from the panic shark.
Intercede and bless my body,
With royal strength of everybody.
I see my friends with outstretched hands,
From home, from church, from outer lands.
All need be done is to accept them,
Concede, allow and simply let them,
Help me find my way to ground,
To healing body, mind that's sound.
Now is their turn as role of healer,
To care for teacher, to be the peeler,
Of last layers of this test, this trauma,
And return to love free of all drama.

Edge of Leaf

Edge of leaf the place between,

Will of wind and tree of green.

Together they will bend and blow,

Prepare themselves for Autumn show.

Display bold colors of truest being,

Inspire all to truest seeing,

Of who we all were born to be,

As timid self sets essence free!

Bruised

Bruised not broken, will heal in time,

Shall double down prayer to hear the Divine.

Listen to Jesus, listen only to Him,

Abolish false gods, seek forgiveness of sin.

For once I allowed healer's voices to reign,

Opinions and guidance all different, none same.

A game of roulette for a sensitive heart,

Time to take back own power, always had from the start!

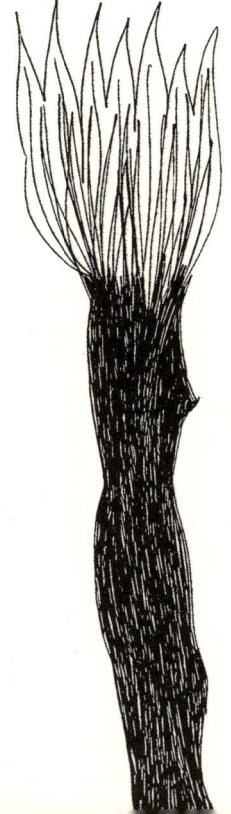

The River

I am, I am the water wide,

Inside my temple two worlds collide.

I am ground of mud and lover's clay,

Where toes may squish and tadpoles play.

I am the place where air meets current,

Fusing elements as nature's servant.

I am, I am God's gracious river,

Peace I offer, healing I deliver.

Chirp, Chirp

"Chirp, chirp the good news of the Lord,"

The parrot squawked, the lion roared!

Blow from the lips sweet bantered quips,

Make merry message for soul's sips.

What fills the ears so fills the heart,

Be bird of bounty who does impart…

Kind song, soft tone of inspiration,

To muse and sing about the nation.

Humming and Healing

Humming and healing to unblock the channel,

Spinal cord of emction in each human mammal.

Allowing the musc es to soften and open,

Allowing the nerves to say what need spoken.

Humble and hopeful they don't take too long,

Praising and prayir g they comeback so strong!

For what the bodies been through it can't be the same,

But it could be even fiercer for soul's given name.

Cracked

When cracked in pieces, broken down,

Let in the light, let in the sound,

OM your way to peaceful nature,

Sun in your center, this I betcha…

Will be the key to open door,

To room of laughs and smile store!

Separate

Separate lives amid same street,

"Why be apart?" the sheep did bleat.

Life's too short to sacrifice,

One's time is meant for paradise.

Heaven on Earth within your reach,

"Be joined and joyful," of this I preach.

Strength of Spirit

Strength of spirit must be the mood,

Faith, family and fortitude.

At the forefront of your mind,

Around the soul protective rind.

Keep it going, keep it up,

Feel wind in face and foot in stirrup.

Soon enough you'll gallop, soon enough you'll run,

Gold horse of God will shine as sun!

A Fairy Flutters

Mending heart beneath the pine,

Consoling with lyric and rhyme,

A fairy flutters in the wood,

Praying he be understood.

A single flame for all to see,

A single flame for all to be,

A smoldering love with mammoth sprawl,

Unbridled, infinite, equal for all.

Go to Him

Go to him,

Fight fog and rain,

Step daisy feet,

To ease his pain.

Skip through his veins,

A buoyant bubble,

Airing out the gloom,

The rubble.

Pour petals on

Crestfallen feet,

Tease toes to twinkle,

Life upbeat.

Fairy blessed to play the part,

Of pixie poet to console a heart.

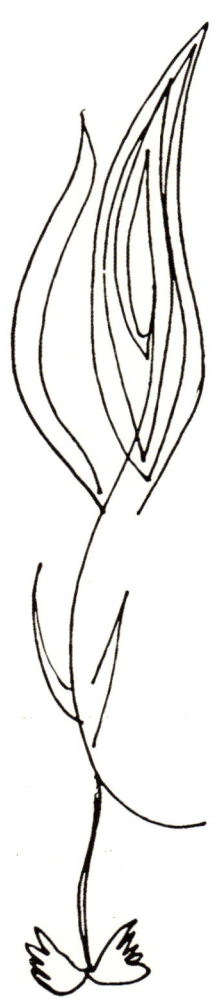

Open Slowly

Open slowly, take your time,

Each petal unfurls in time of Divine.

Do not rush, don't lag behind,

Pace of grace for peace of mind.

Patience is the teacher now,

Lay it all down and take a bow,

Unto your Maker, unto the Earth,

The elements will enhance your birth.

Water, fire, air and stone,

Surround yourself 'til deep in bone,

You feel them seep, remove the weep,

You feel them fill, wipe up the spill.

For nature is your truest friend,

When body is in need of mend.

Love Abounds

Love abounds amidst the trauma,

Love will rise, banish the drama,

For love heals all and God's the dealer,

For love within, our truest healer.

Mother Mary

Mother Mary, whisper soft,
How may I serve the empty loft?
Breeze comfort cross the windowsill,
Lightness of being through his locale.

Form me into fairy orb,
To slide beneath the crack in door.
Bounce about the walls with glee,
Stamping call of humility.

Keep Me

Keep me humble, keep me whole,

Keep me on the path to know.

Without God I am but bones,

A kaleidoscope of sticks and stones.

God is the force, the Highest Order,

In His charge, I shall not shoulder,

Careless whispers of the ego,

Believing in its dark tuxedo.

In truth I am but of a veil,

Between Earth's crown and heaven's tail.

A slip of sunshine to bring light,

To God's perfection, His ultimate Might.

Humble Him

Be meek in manner,

Yet strong in word.

Stand eye to eye,

You shall be heard.

Guard your heart,

From rant and rumble,

Desired outcome,

To heal and humble.

Bring gift of petal,

Penance and poem,

God's light, God's love,

Presence of home.

Party Crasher

He crashed my party,

And kissed my soul.

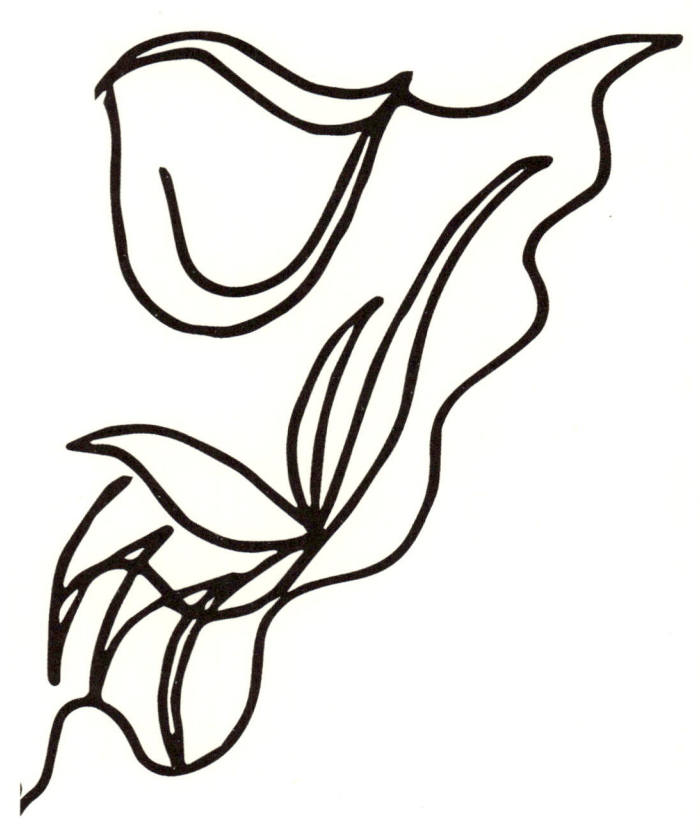

Molar of Lies

Molar of lies in mouth of man,

Must be extracted by truth's hand.

Accused

Accused of tryst and/or affair,

Due to strength of spirit pair.

It is not I the girl of call,

And yet some-how I take the fall.

My heart is pure and oh too wise,

To ever allow compromise,

Of virtue, truth and harmony,

For man's desired fruit of tree.

Hushed Heart

Ba dump, Ba dump!

Pitter, patter, pound and pump!

Lovesick paddles shock hushed heart,

Flip a circuit, toss a dart,

Pierce a coat of claws and spikes,

Worn to shun the looks and likes.

Best to stay off playing field,

Craft a romance safety shield.

Keep head above a rising tide,

Keep self from love, the water wide.

Refuse to fall and be held captive,

By feelings sometimes vast, reactive.

Yet all will face that fateful day,

When one appears to crack dense clay,

Peel back the onion, disrobe the armor,

Play role of amorous snake charmer.

Hook 'em

Hook him with a wink, a smile,

Lure him in with feminine wile,

As rod does bend to point of break,

Snag him out of Canyon Lake.

Into a boat of sugar and spice,

Ribbons and bows, white Edelweiss.

Harbor heart in space and hand,

Offering soft place to land.

Free him of the captive line,

Struggle no more so says the Divine.

Time has come to meet his mate,

The yin to yang of equal gate.

Girl shower him a splish, a splash,

With drops of grace and drops of sass.

Flirt and flaunt sweet summer soul,

Blast yellow rays that live below,

Supple limbs and torrid tones,

Rose scented skin and breezy bones.

Be queen to king for grand finale,

Dig deep inside your honey valley.

Victress to victor of healing and light,

Bequile the man, assert your birthright.

Satin weave on magic loom,

God's tapestry of groom to womb.

Clarity

Humble the heart.

Straighten the road,

Simplify need,

Love shall be sowed.

Fall Easy

Fall easy to the wonder,

Carefree of plight or plunder,

Make moonstruck love and sled the sun,

Succumb to the awaited one.

Beamed

Musical note floated midair,

Escaped the knots of tangled snare,

Monogrammed with letter J,

Waited for like friend to play.

Crashed down from cloud, staccato note,

Primed for fun, set to emote,

The need to strum a song and sing,

Visit park, fly high on swing.

Make aware the call to partner,

Be to the other sincere gardener.

Life's rhythm set or so it seemed

Until God's will said notes be beamed.

Healing

Healing in motion, body knows what to do,

'Tis been waiting for heart assist from you.

Stay open and loving, trusting and true,

To the practice that saved you when you were blue.

Again, yoga will be your friend not your foe,

Onward now, be not afraid to let go,

Within the four corners of your sage green mat,

Feel safe to explore the this and the that,

Of movement, of breath, of tears and of smiles,

Of laughter, of foibles, of courage that dials,

Up to the max volume just because you showed up,

To begin again in hopes to disrupt,

Fear pattern that snatched you from love's rocking hammock,

Always comes the day when we no longer can stand it.

We roll out our mat, step foot on its rubber,

Center ourselves among one another.

Trust and believe in the holy power,

Of spirit's comeback through vinyasa breath shower.

Love Your Neighbor

Love your neighbor, forgive your friend,

Times such as these are meant to mend,

Bitter feuds, senseless grudges,

The Holy Spirit often nudges,

Us to grow from separation,

Make reuniting our destination.

Now let it go and let it be,

Repair the damage, restore family.

Yesteryear

Were you here in yesteryear,

With woman that you held so dear?

Were you here about the fountain,

Asking her to marry mountain?

Were you here in city street,

Taking plunge of lover's leap?

Were you here in Windy City,

Confusing her for me, oh pity.

Snow Globe

Was living life just as I wished,

Buzzing through the days and lists,

Endless chores, phone calls and meetings,

Taking for granted in person greetings.

How was I to know one day?

In the blink of an eye, it be taken away.

Home I would be to sit with self,

Ponder this hand that I'd been dealt.

Dig deep to see what I am made of,

In times of strife and withheld love.

Find in my center a cushion of calm,

A spirit of hope, a mind that is strong.

At time my snow globe flipped and shaken,

Are times of growth and for the taken…

Time to see what truly matters,

Before glass breaks and snow globe shatters.

I pray this world will join in sentiment,

Or fear our planet and the detriment,

That can occur when we're not together,

For when we are one, we are for the better.

Easy Does It

Easy does it, get your rest,

Still weeks are needed til at your best.

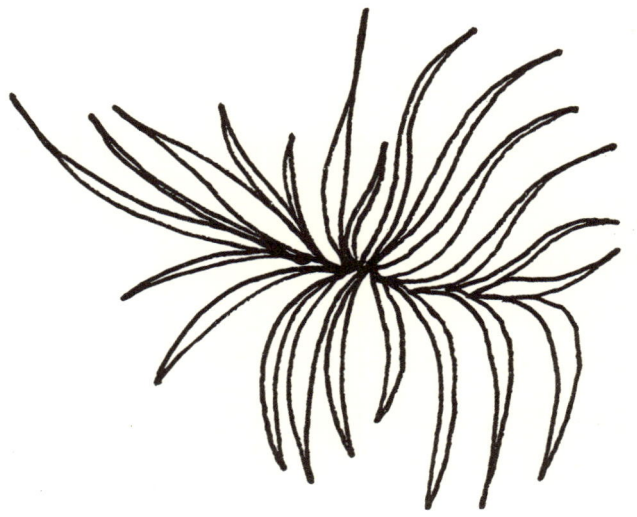

Hiccup

Bewildered eyes right from the start,

Volcanic hiccup of the heart.

What's one to do when in walks love?

The rare and missing matching glove.

Run like hell or face the truth?

Been searching for this soul since youth.

Paralyzed, how can this be?

It's not the time or place to see,

They do exist, they are for real,

Your sanity they're sure to steal.

Love at first sight, a wild ride,

Forevermore no chance to hide,

Behind old stories, lies, excuses,

Suddenly life introduces,

All that you've been looking for,

Equality and then some more.

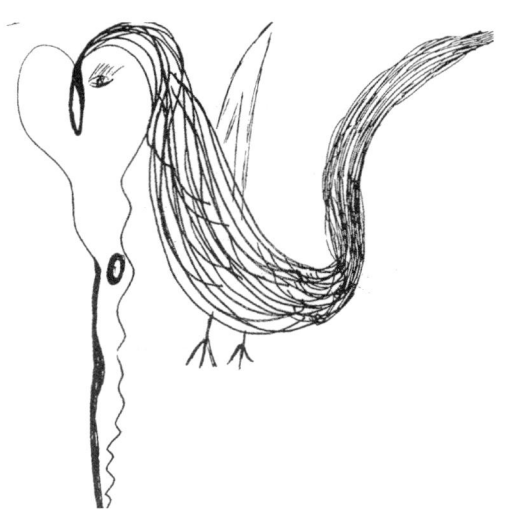

Wild Horse

Unleashed, unbridled, un-tame, unkempt,
Love's wild horse to tease and tempt,
Black stallion hiding in his stable,
Gun-shy to roam in romance fable.

Safe in hay of love gone wrong,
Straw of risk tickles too strong,
Trough of heartbreak fills to brim,
Reminding self he just can't win.

Damned if you do, damned if you don't,
Masquerade of will and won't,
Spiral of the ups and downs,
The pits of partners, the milestone crowns.

Take a breath you noble steed,
Not every union makes you bleed.
Press through the gate and run new race,
With equal equine, in true about face.

Run Wild

Run wild, run free,

Unafraid to ride the river with me.

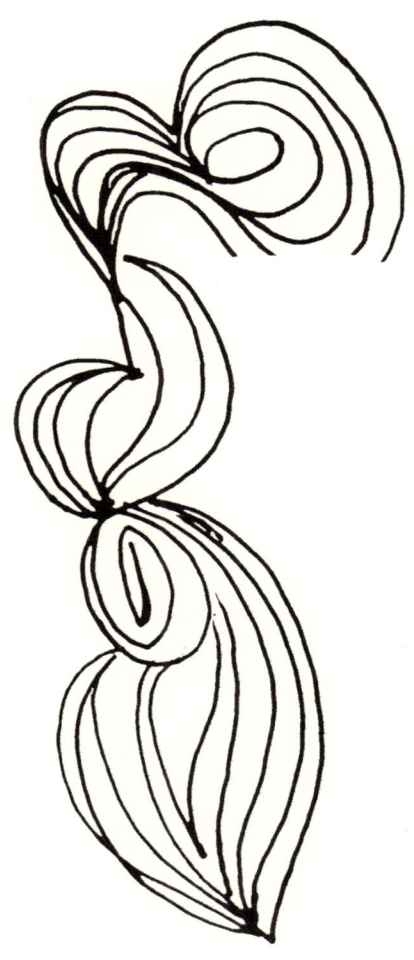

The Moment

Who is this guy inspecting me?

No connoisseur of who I be.

Inquisitive about my worth,

Size and shape, origin on Earth.

Seems concerned if I'm the one,

Rubs me between finger, thumb.

Smirks then sighs a gentle breath,

Recognized this welcome death.

An era will end and one will begin,

As decision is made and I am to win,

A front row seat to surprise and glee,

Bear witness to love's bended knee.

A yelp, a gasp and tears of joy,

As girl says yes to lucky boy!

Wedding Bells

Big love, small affair,

Wedding day without fanfare.

It's not a production, but a promise,

Rings of wings to join the amorous.

Gold Together

Gold together, gold apart,

The shimmer of two, a metallic dart,

A spike to spark and wake the world,

Planet be purified, people be pearled.

The command, the call from up above,

Release the doves, surrender love.

Flip Flop

Flip flop, cherry top,

Have found the one who makes heart POP!

Pulse and pump, flutter, fool,

This old soul to bray like mule.

"Hee-haw, hee-haw!" in poet rhyme,

An ass for love of the Divine.

Cheers!

Inside the logs of lost love's past,

One cup of wine, one whiskey glass,

A cheers to end the tears and rage,

A book to offer crisp clean page.

To sketch fresh portrait, write new story,

Beyond all bounds of category.

To take a leap and fly like dove,

Soar toward once in a lifetime love.

Sanctified

Christ sanctified the skin, the bone,

Illuminated aura shone,

Upon each bird and fellow man,

Big medicine to heal the land.

AWAKE

Awake

Here I am where it all began,

Deep in tree bark, taking a stand,

Safe and sound in feet made fertile,

Care no longer to run his circle.

Heritage of Emerald Isle,

Esteem, demeanor far from mild.

Woman a wolf with righteous howl,

To eradicate man's deadly prowl.

Slide of hand, indiscreet suggestion,

Untoward behavior called into question.

For did he not know from the strength of her prose,

Never to reckon with a wild Irish rose.

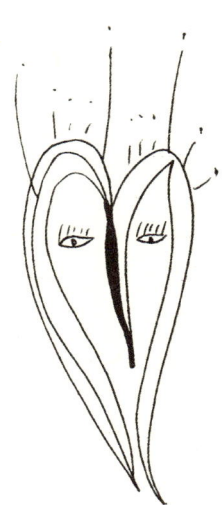

The Bell

Ding Dong the bell for me,
Unique to him I'll never be.
A flowered patch on applique,
Solely a sprig of the cortege.

Wake up dear one and know your worth,
Stand firm in God, reclaim your mirth.
Poise redeemed from the hypnotic,
Mind revived you are exotic.

Love the Skin You're In

Love the skin you're in,

The prickly parts, the sheepish grin,

Birthmarks and scars from sibling battles,

Hearts flips and flutters, hearts shake's and rattles.

Worn out work feet, dishpan hands,

Evidence you're not in the stands,

But on the field of life and courage,

Playing the play to lift, encourage,

All those around you in world you need,

To get back in game and take own lead.

Ants are Marching

Ants are marching, squirrels a buzz,

Caterpillars jumping fuzz!

Woodpeckers knocking, "Now's the time,"

Be blinding sun of carefree shine.

Owl hoots song pure and wise,

You're so much bigger than your size.

Mighty buck stands at attention,

Observing you with satisfaction.

Turtle Tracks

Riding along on the tip of a tail,

Of a turtle with pace slower than snail.

Hopped onto her shell, an intricate maze,

Of pathways and alleys etched from sad, dark days.

From life lessons, conditions, arduous and extreme,

Carvings and caverns from soul's repressed scream.

Followed each trail, some rocky dead end,

Had to turn back, try again and again,

To find my way forward, to find my way home,

Skip through muddled jungle to clarity home.

Stepped off the shell to a clear and bright head,

Warrior of light once laden with lead.

Opened third eye, indigo sail and mast,

Conquered the labyrinth of hearts heavy past.

Allowed eye to guide me in the right direction,

Intuition the captain replacing perfection.

The journey took time, we all have our own rhythm,

Our mistakes and our blunders, we have to forgive them.

Heart of a Lion

Buckled breast safeguards a settle,

Heart of a lion, heart of a petal.

Hear her roar, witness her bloom,

Thrashing out of bygone's womb.

At Your Feet

At Your feet where I belong,

Wrapped in humility sarong.

Amazing grace you have bestowed,

Upon this heart once undertowed,

By weight of world and reckless choice,

Now time to heed only God's voice.

Touched

Touched by the Lord,

To strike a peace chord,

Unite an army,

With a truth sword.

Collect your birds,

Each one a treasure,

Made for purpose,

And or pleasure.

Together you shall fly My route,

You in the lead to bring about,

A spark, a fire, a transformation,

A joyful movement, a holy foundation.

Unique

You've made me unique and I'm grateful to be,

Yet there seems no right place that understands me.

Where am I to take the gifts you've bestowed?

The weight and the waiting are one heavy load.

I Rise

I rise to walk the path of Christ,

Follow the signs of gifted sight,

Seeds of truth to sow each step,

This call to joy I do accept.

Baptism by Fire

Baptism by fire the only way,

To cleanse the palette, prepare you to say,

Out loud to the world just who you are,

God's poet and girl with deep battle scar.

The trauma you've suffered has taught you compassion,

Letting go and listening to your intuition.

Welcome new role as author and speaker,

Is meant to bring comfort to those who feel weaker.

And yet you will tell them they as strong as you,

That you also have suffered as they now do.

Give hope to the weary, strength to the frail,

Love to the lonely, your heart be the sail,

That catches the wind and carries them through,

The ocean of waves, size never they knew,

Could possibly hit them and yet they still did,

Life tests us all, on that you can bid,

All your chips, all your fortune,

We all feel a torchin'.

It is then we find out what we're truly made of,

Who are our real friends that we can speak of.

Although it will seem the tunnel too dark,

Christ be the light at the end to stoke spark.

The Day Has Come

The day has come, my chicks have grown,

And from home's nest for they have flown,

What is my purpose now to be?

No more routine to face daily.

Only one answer came to mind,

Felt oh so grateful I no longer blind,

To the amazing grace bestowed on me,

By Christ the King, the Lord of thee.

So once upon a sunny day,

I lay my body down to pray,

Gave my body over to God,

For his purpose my feet now trod.

Approach

Fan your tail feather, fluff your chest,

Own feminine power, begin you quest.

Make your move, up your game,

Time no longer to be tame.

A new approach you are to take,

Integrity is now at stake.

Step in and share how much you care,

Rescue him from liar's lair.

Lead the Charge

You have nothing to lose, nothing to hide,

Fear not and surrender to God's wild ride.

Boulders moved to clear the path,

Lead the charge, God's got your back.

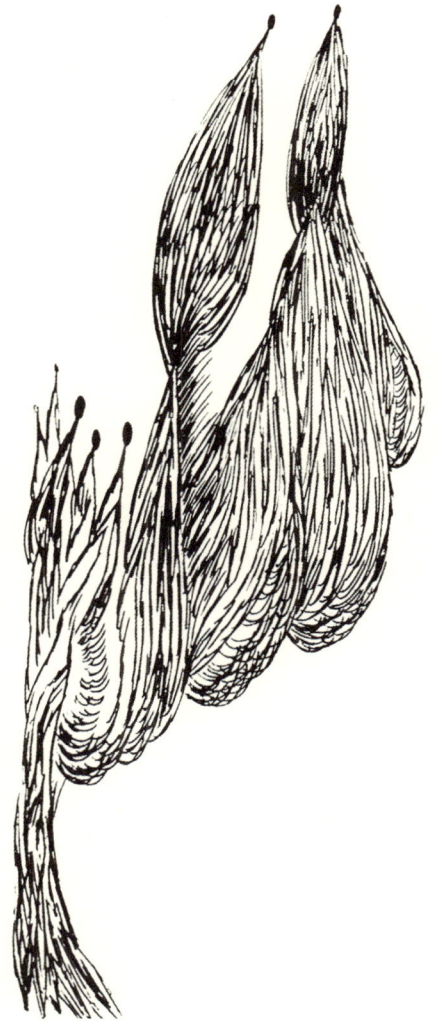

Knock 'em Down

Knock 'em down, know 'em dead,

Truth be told you fill his head.

Stand down, stand firm, stand up, stand-off,

Worthy to drink from the same trough.

For can't you see and don't you know,

He looked for you so long ago.

In his despair of seek, no find,

He settled heart to quiet mind.

Married another to cure and net,

His restless soul that was beset,

By the one, the girl, the dream, the truth,

Who light lassoed soft heart of youth.

Scamper Man

Scamper man can't you stand still,

Face equal woman, challenge, thrill?

Thrust self in pot of true belonging,

Twinkle the keys of deepest longing.

Teeter-Totter

There comes a point at which you know,

One friend does reap more than they sow.

The teeter-totter never even,

One up in air as they're mistreatin'.

Soul up in sky, soul down below,

Directing arrow of the bow.

Reciprocity a mouse,

Nonexistent in wheel house.

Some parks of life are not worth staying,

Game will end when you stop playing.

Face Off

The day has come, the time is near,

To face abuser without fear.

Hold my own and calmly speak,

Of trials that made my heart leak.

Forgive the deeds, yet no longer follow,

Teaching and words soured and hollow.

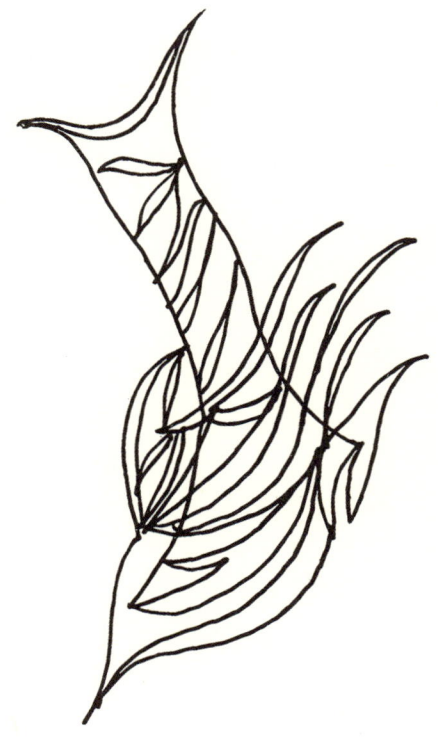

Devoted Daisy

Simple, friendly is her way,

To brighten any forest's day.

Crisp clean petals white as snow,

Her yellow eye is in the know.

Gently gazing through the brush,

Witnessing woods never rush.

She sees the trees all work together,

As gingerly as floating feather.

Each blade of grass, each clump of mud,

Has purpose from The Lord above.

Plays its part to equalize,

No matter of its tiny size.

And there she stems among the weeds,

The fallen acorns, the buried seeds.

Her only job to simply be.

Her truest self for all to see.

In doing so she plays a hand,

In shining truth throughout the land.

Some fellow flowers think her crazy,

She's simply a devoted daisy.

The Reckoning

Was called to stand in total truth,

Rise from my seat of silence booth,

Speak the secrets, face the glare,

Of recipient's intense dark stare.

Heed

I wake in night to heed the call,

Supported by the pups, the Fall,

If a tree can bear to bare itself,

Then so shall I reveal myself.

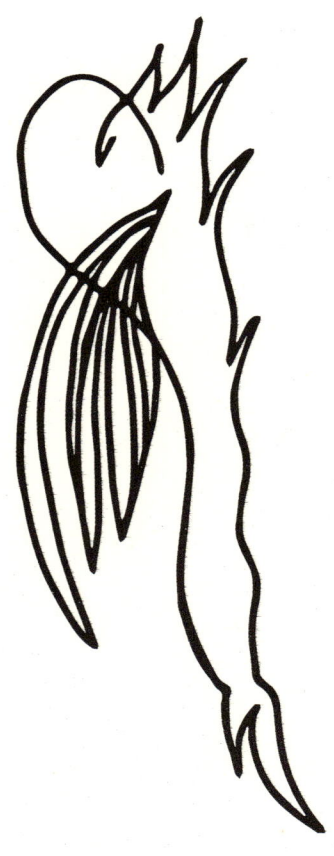

Snug as a Bug

Snug as a bug in smallest self,

She hid her gifts, God's given wealth.

Would rather curl up in a ball,

Than to be seen standing up tall.

For who is she to lead the way?

Best to keep those skills at bay.

Play it small and keep life simple,

To play it big a risky dimple.

In a soul who's always fought,

Her strength and power which can't be bought.

Yet now it's time to face the truth,

Step into role of leader, sleuth,

Discover what is possible,

Allow herself be watchable,

Break open the cocoon of shame,

Shine bright and claim her right to fame.

Not fame of fortune or of limelight,

But fame of doing what is right.

Refusing to turn a blind eye,

To those in need, to those that lie.

Be not a woman of frosty glass,

But clear, transparent, a real bad-ass!

Light it Up

Light it up, purge the past,

Time to shine has come at last!

Be not timid, you've earned your stripes,

Be not shaken by groans and gripes.

Of those who've yet to take the leap,

'Tis not your job to carry heap.

Nor burden barrel of opinion,

Drink only from the Lord's dominion.

Dive In

Dive in and swim the worldly waters,

Oceans of cultured sons and daughters.

Splash your fin, flip your flippers,

Stave off the wretched devil quivers.

Shed yesteryears sad scales of blue,

Be sparkle fish of ra nbow hue.

Turn grey waters purple, green,

Air gills of joy to ma<e them gleam!

Remind the seas of people please,

To expose their colors with grace and ease.

Shine A Light

Shine a light, tis your birthright,

To be as bright as sun's delight!

Worry not of other's pinch,

Of those who carry heart of Grinch.

'Tis not concern for you to bear,

You've earned the right to let down hair.

Expose the truth, bare the soul,

Freedom be the holy goal.

Emerge

Emerge into a being of light,

An angel born to take Christ's flight.

Lands of adventure He's sending you to,

Spread the joy of the Lord as only you do.

Pop!

Cluster of bubbles to surface did pop!

Some shocking, some painful, each one put a stop,

To the blister inside me of which I didn't cause,

Was under the reign of man's chosen laws.

"Trains leaving the tunnel, get on or get off,"

His reply to my inquiry at which he did scoff.

No interest was shown in my side of the story,

Was his way or no way for train trip to glory.

Oh contraire my treasured friend,

The things I say are meant to mend.

For you to hear, to listen, receive,

All come from heart, you must believe.

A messenger God's made of me,

To fly with grace, humility,

Into your world as truthful dove,

To see your struggle with only love.

The Dancing Flower

Dawn dipped through windows, lit the wall,

Bullets of rainbows spread big and small,

Morning delight made for the mystic,

Tis said wild rose be shamanistic.

Gift of color, gift of God,

Cracked every pore, a lightning rod.

Consumed with glory,

Held by grace,

Skin became Chantilly lace.

Mane of gold a waterfall,

Feet pink slippers whispered call,

To leap and prance, twist and twirl,

Be every inch a fairy girl.

Greet morning with a pirouette,

Worship God with silhouette.

Lift holy heart and hands to Him,

Trust course of day unto His whim,

Take hold of self and feminine power,

In service as the dancing flower.

Old Friends

Old friends can never be replaced,

The laughs you've shared, the trials you've faced,

No matter the miles that run between them,

Their hearts connect again and again.

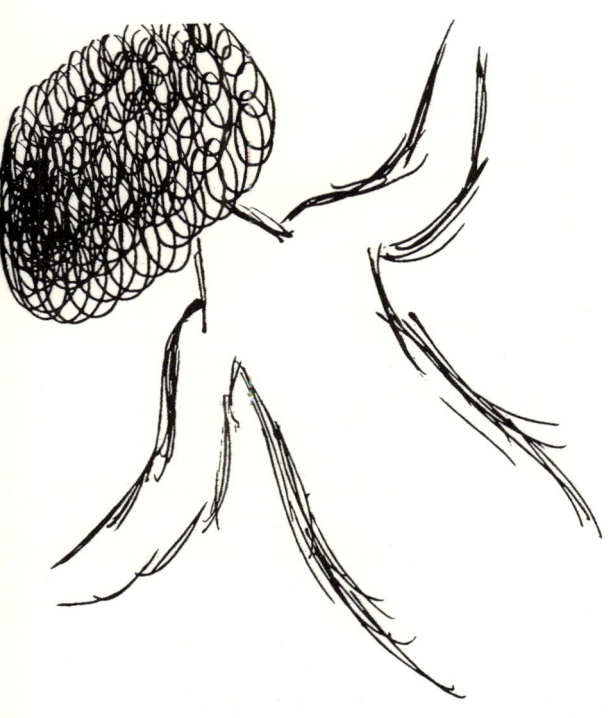

Feminine Fortress

Feminine fortress to harbor a seed,

Cleansed by the Spirit for purpose and deed,

To bring forth a baby of ancestor's past,

There's no turning back, the dye has been cast.

Holy Baby

Holy baby of my heart,

Blessed by Christ to play the part,

In joining two who never knew,

True union 'til they both outgrew,

Being stuck in same old place,

Patterns, habits, war-torn space.

Despair, disease and all it brings,

Until a breaking of the strings.

Suddenly, wide open field,

To harvest love, lay down fear shield.

Free at last to raise the bar,

To be exactly who they are.

Ready

Ready to see, ready to stand,

Ready to share holy light in the hand.

Hidden Acres

Hidden acres of story's below,

How was I to ever know?

One day to surface they would break,

Life as I knew it would be at stake.

Turnabout

Bloodied words coughed up and out,

Had been waiting for the turnabout,

Of a woman who they knew once wild,

From birth to toddler to tenacious child.

A tomboy, twister, true hellcat,

In trees she climbed, at rules she spat!

Small in size with so much to say,

Deep down she knew there would come a day,

To let it fly, release the kraken,

Answer the call and let it happen.

Make her move, leave her mark,

Around the world she will embark.

Tell a story, live her truth,

Lift God's people, raise the roof!

Halt

Still your feet, become like air,

Wind as a whip for pore's prepare,

To soak in heaven's angel mist,

Amazing grace of God's pure kiss.

Delivery

It came to be upon the river,

Time had come for Christ's deliver,

Me unto selected people,

To charge the works of joy and steeple.

A holy call of passion, mercy,

To heal the hungry, quench the thirsty,

To live among the poor, the lonely,

To serve the suffering in His name only.

Paint the Keys

Paint the keys with strings of deeds,

Cast a spell for world to tell,

Of the merry song that we all belong,

To one another and The Holy Mother,

To Son of host and The Holy Ghost,

In God our Father, find no bother,

Receive only glory and endless love,

From heavens kingdom up above.

Crossroads

Alone in plains of country road,

In contemplation of love sowed.

I stood the crossroads, the intersection,

Pondering next step, direction.

Four paths resembled former teachers,

Who lifted me to loge from bleachers.

Yet on this day no step felt right,

Streets not needed for my sight.

Old routes no longer filling cup,

My feet grew buds and sprouted up!

Here-in-after go straight to Source,

Let light of God declare the course.

Shoot from the Hip

Shoot from the hip, you'll figure it out,

Make stumbles and fumbles until it works out,

Things always do given ample time,

And follow your heart and universe sign.

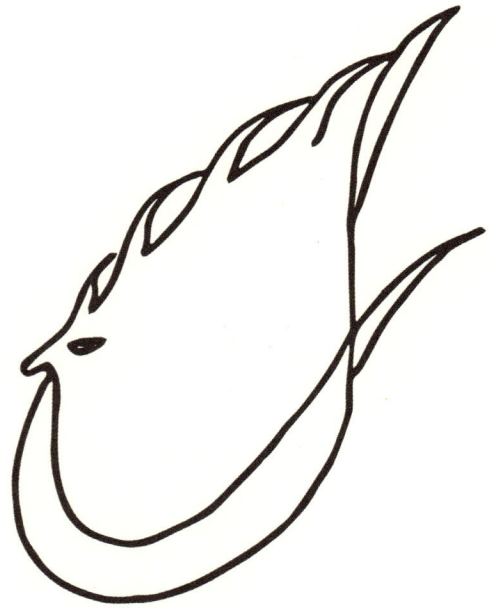

The Hummingbird

The magic of a hummingbird,

Lies within her belly curve.

Inside her center a precious stone,

A dazzling emerald all her own.

A sea of green to lift up hearts,

Repair soul wounds, gift them fresh starts.

In flight she vibrates owning aura,

At rest she nestles in nature's flora.

Cleansing and restoring self,

So she may thrive and share her wealth.

Daffodil Leader

Today I smelled a daffodil,

Scent of a leader gave me chill,

First bloom of Spring, color of yellow,

Inspiration hue for fellow.

Shape of a speaker, a megaphone,

Blasts out, "Wake up! Come out of home,"

For Spring is here, so much to see,

The busy bird, the budding tree.

The fertile soil an offering,

For growth, new life, may freedom ring!

My love, my love

My love, my love, for all my life,

I've longed to be your loving wife.

At first, I did not know it you,

Who was the perfect fitting shoe.

Friends we were and friends we'd be,

Through thick and thin til bended knee.

For finally came the day we shifted,

From friend to fiancé, a treasure gifted.

When this veil is lifted, when this storm has passed,

Marriage will bind us at long last.

And on that day, strength of our bond,

Will take us places far beyond,

What we have known in days of past,

As man and wife, the die be cast,

What God has joined no one shall separate,

Til death do us part, my soul is yours, an open gate.

Jump the Fence

Jump the fence to brighter pasture,

Awaits a field of well-earned stature.

Obedience to God you've shown,

And in return how much you've grown.

Wide open spaces so you crave,

Room to buck and misbehave!

Whinny to the winds of change,

"I'm ready for adventure's range!"

Breakaway

Black coals reside in back of mind,
Remnants of the push and grind.
Last bit of me to finally burn,
Surrender self and make the turn,

Around the bend, last leg of race,
On track of past shall leave no trace.
Time has come to breakaway,
Sprint by the old for future day.

Rid the soul of former stories,
Make space for cleaner, clearer quarries.
Cleanse the palette of poor taste,
Left in the mouth from those two-faced.

Hit your stride, don't look back,
Toward all you bear, not what you lack.
Sure-footed in each step of thunder,
Heart of fortitude and wonder!

White Tornado

A flurry of feathers formed a cyclone,

White tornado of truth about to be born!

Whirled through a town once thought to be clean,

Washed dirty laundry of what now had been seen.

Intent not to harm, solely set secrets free,

Air the body and mind of weight canopy.

Heal fallen fellows who felt same affliction,

Under regime of human condition.

Embark

Embark to every plain and shore,
To those with less who do care more,
About such love with no condition,
Where all are one with no partition.

The poor are rich in fellowship,
Stripped of ego, showmanship.
Pure in heart, scarce in word,
Eyes tell story of unheard.

Visit lands in need of plenty,
Beginning in year 2020.
Scout the way to pave the path,
Each step toward righteous aftermath.

Center of Self

In the center of the self, the gut,

A yellow light does glow for but,

Ourselves to harness our own power,

Shoot rays of light top of each hour!

Fill the world with inspiration,

So other souls reach destination,

Of their own light inside to shine,

Given at birth by the Divine.

For the Lord

I am of the Lord and for the Lord,

An angel of His own discord.

To live the day as He see fit,

Sun up to down, I shall not quit.

Will tread the water dark and rough,

Climb any mountain deemed to too tough.

Walk through land of plague and sorrow,

Gift to all brighter tomorrow.

Fire, Fire!

Fire, fire fill my legs,
Skyrocket me so body begs!
Into the role of healer, mystic,
Into a woman altruistic.

Oh wandering soul and spirit free,
Time has come to let all be.
Immerse yourself unto Thy calling,
Eradicate habit of stalling.

Grateful to God

Grateful to God for saving me,

From self, from devil, from tethered tree.

Allowing me to have the chance,

To write own tale of circumstance.

To offer a release through pen,

To open door of lion's den.

Be free of idols and other's voices,

Be free to make own healthy choices.

Thank you Christ for amazing grace,

Please paint your peace upon my face.

Flying

Flying into something new,

Often daunting thing to do.

Take your time, glide and circle,

Surveying view of pink and purple,

Sunrises, sunsets, blue waters calm,

Each one a poem and holy psalm.

Look down on trees, carpet of green,

Heart of the Earth, strong and serene.

Gaze upon the beasts and humans,

Knowing one thing is for certain,

We all have impact on one another,

All come from Source, one for the other.

Foundation of Birds

When love walks in, then love walks out,
Be not shaken by sad bout,
For always round the corner waits,
Another soul that satiates,
The longing of your heart and hopes,
A partner to walk the tight ropes,
Of building something fresh and new,
Forming foundation for those blue.
For those who feel there is no hope,
For those who no longer can cope.
In ye shall fly to fill their cup,
Bounty of love sure to disrupt,
The grief, despair, the loss, the pain,
The wheel they've run yet all in vain.
For who to heal better than birds?
With cheerful songs, uplifting words.
In service under God's employ,
Time to be missionary of joy!
Wear your costumes, flap about,
Clear foggy air with silly sprout.
This world needs nonsense to tickle bones,
This world craves laughter and happy homes.
Use graceful gifts and unique traits,
To walk the poor through plenty gates.
Give them a roof, a bed, a dream,
Give them a smile they've never seen.
In concert you will all find peace,
At once your pasts shall all release.
At last the second act begins,
A balanced axis finally spins.
In one another new family formed,
Warriors who've weathered storm.

Stilts

Enough with the crutches,

It's time for the stilts!

God, Saints, Angels, Dad...

Lead me where I am to go,

Fill my cup and watch me grow!

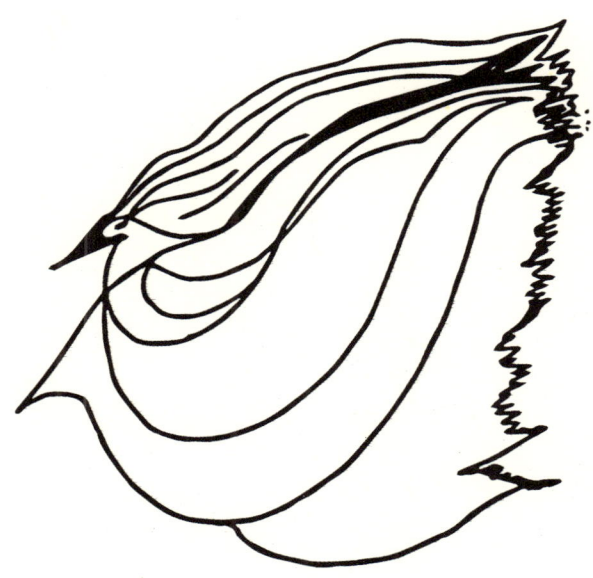

ABOUT THE AUTHOR

I am

I am a lover of the trees,

Of flowers, God, of kindness deeds.

A poet of the truth I see,

When unafraid to let things be.

Nature's heart my previous muse,

To fill my cup and light a fuse,

To serve, to love, to teach, to heal,

To live, to laugh, to keep it real.

Lisa Kahl